Milnaa is the first Contextual Collaboration place where individuals and businesses can get work done, network, and learn while having fun— all at their own pace.

Sign up now to improve the quality and efficiency of personal and business collaborations:
https://www.milnaa.com/

Contextual Collaborations!

The Future of Work and Play Where You Can Do More for Less

Steve Sudhir Chainani

Foreword by
Mitchell Levy, The AHA Guy

THiNKaha®

An Actionable Business Journal

E-mail: info@thinkaha.com
20660 Stevens Creek Blvd., Suite 210
Cupertino, CA 95014

Published by THiNKaha®
20660 Stevens Creek Blvd., Suite 210, Cupertino, CA 95014
http://thinkaha.com
E-mail: info@thinkaha.com

First Printing: February 2018
Hardcover ISBN: 978-1-61699-240-8 1-61699-240-9
Paperback ISBN: 978-1-61699-239-2 1-61699-239-5
eBook ISBN: 978-1-61699-238-5 1-61699-238-7
Place of Publication: Silicon Valley, California, USA
Paperback Library of Congress Number: 2017961104

Trademarks

All terms mentioned in this book that are known to be trademarks or service marks have been appropriately capitalized. Neither THiNKaha, nor any of its imprints, can attest to the accuracy of this information. Use of a term in this book should not be regarded as affecting the validity of any trademark or service mark.

Warning and Disclaimer

Every effort has been made to make this book as complete and as accurate as possible. The information provided is on an "as is" basis. The author(s), publisher, and their agents assume no responsibility for errors or omissions. Nor do they assume liability or responsibility to any person or entity with respect to any loss or damages arising from the use of information contained herein.

Acknowledgement & Dedication

This book is dedicated to my entire team that helped develop the concept of Contextual Collaboration as the Future of Work. Special gratitude to Mitchell Levy, Harrison Turner, Bhawna Bajaj, Juber Khan, and Maharishi Desai. Further encouragement from Priyanka Bassi and my parents, Vic and Shirley Chainani, as well as team Milnaa.com for their vision and commitment as I formulated my prognostications on the Evolution of Work.

How to Read a THiNKaha® Book

A Note from the Publisher

The THiNKaha series is the CliffsNotes of the 21st century. The value of these books is that they are contextual in nature. Although the actual words won't change, their meaning will change every time you read one as your context will change. Experience your own "AHA!" moments ("AHAmessages™") with a THiNKaha book; AHAmessages are looked at as "actionable" moments—think of a specific project you're working on, an event, a sales deal, a personal issue, etc. and see how the AHAmessages in this book can inspire your own AHAmessages, something that you can specifically act on. Here's how to read one of these books and have it work for you:

1. Read a THiNKaha book (these slim and handy books should only take about 15–20 minutes of your time!) and write down one to three actionable items you thought of while reading it. Each journal-style THiNKaha book is equipped with space for you to write down your notes and thoughts underneath each AHAmessage.

2. Mark your calendar to re-read this book again in 30 days.

3. Repeat step #1 and write down one to three more AHAmessages that grab you this time. I guarantee that they will be different than the first time. BTW: this is also a great time to reflect on the actions taken from the last set of AHAmessages you wrote down.

After reading a THiNKaha book, writing down your AHAmessages, re-reading it, and writing down more AHAmessages, you'll begin to see how these books contextually apply to you. THiNKaha books advocate for continuous, lifelong learning. They will help you transform your ahas into actionable items with tangible results until you no longer have to say "AHA!" to these moments—they'll become part of your daily practice as you continue to grow and learn.

As The AHA Guy at THiNKaha, I definitely practice what I preach. I read 2-3 AHAbooks a month in addition to those that we publish and take away two to three different action items from each of them every time. Please e-mail me your AHAs today!

Mitchell Levy
publisher@thinkaha.com

Contents

Foreword
by Mitchell Levy, The AHA Guy at AHAthat and TEDx Speaker

Human beings are social creatures. We are tribal in nature. In the agricultural age, collaboration was a key component of survival. The butcher, baker, and candlestick maker would collaborate to share each other's products.

As we moved into cities, collaboration decreased with the evolution into factories and the optimization of processes. We focused more on improving factory performance than on family collaboration. Management took a command-and-control approach, where there was a leader and a set of followers. The followers didn't collaborate, they followed orders. Work was work and for most, not fun.

As we transition into the social age, we're seeing collaboration brought back into the fold. We have an opportunity to create an environment for humans where work is something we want to do, when we want to do it, and where we want to do it. This can happen if we focus on collaboration—not just between humans and humans, but also between humans and computers.

With increasing computing power and functionality, we're seeing great strides in artificial intelligence, video conferencing, and collaborative tools. A common theme in these apps is an increased focus on collaboration that's very contextual in nature. Technology allows us to extend our multi-faceted interests beyond our small community. We can now interact in areas of work and play with those of similar interests from around the world.
Many have already recognized the value of the collective. Wikipedia is a great example of this. Going forward, the collective voice will permeate into all we do.

Steve Sudhir Chainani understands this trend and addresses this movement in his book, *Contextual Collaborations!* We are just at the beginning of a massive shift in how we live, work, and play. Pay attention to contextual collaboration, as it will play an important component in this transformation.

Introduction

The evolving world of creation, production, and services will be unrecognizable from where we stand today. In other words, the meaning of "Work" will morph into an unrecognizable paradigm. Concomitantly, "Play" will evolve—we will have much more time for recreation and play than we dare imagine today. Robots, Internet of Things, and Deep Learning machines will run most of our current work activities. What is science fiction today will be tomorrow's reality.

Embrace the impending paradigm shift and be mentally prepared while increasing your technological skills. The world will be driven by technology.

Prognostications on the Evolution of WORK"

"An activity involving mental or physical effort, done in order to achieve a purpose or result."

"Mental or physical activity done to earn an income or a living."

Work is constantly in a state of flux. The only constant in the universe is change. The world we live in is changing at an astounding rate. We are at the early stages of a revolution so big that our universally accepted paradigms of today will be unrecognizable in a mere 20 years.

So, what is this change, you may ask?

It's been a mere twenty-two years since the internet became available to average folk. The Netscape browser made it possible to surf the net, send email, and shop. In the past twenty-two years, the internet has become central to almost every activity we do on a daily basis. Our telephones have become "smart" and "portable." They are our primary gateway to the world.

Doing "WORK" now has an additional meaning: "sharing, networking, documenting, communicating, ideating, and producing economic value by pressing keys on a smartphone or laptop computer." That's just my definition. Do you agree?
Yes, we get paid now to do the above . . . it's now the largest segment of our digital economy and growing by leaps and bounds. The top five companies in the United States by market capitalization are all tech leaders: Apple, Google, Microsoft, Amazon, and Facebook. They are all involved in making people more productive in their personal or business lives.

As India's spiritual leader, Mahatma Gandhi, once famously said, "Become the change you want to see." Are we now ready for stupendous change?

The next decade will see tens of millions of traditional jobs disappear. Robots will do most factory jobs. Service bots, artificial intelligence-based systems, will automatically do jobs that well-educated people do today. For instance, most medical diagnoses will be done at home via a "thinking" device and a transducer placed under your tongue. In a few short seconds, you will know precisely what ails you. All your medical records and prescription drugs will be on the cloud. Visits to a medical practitioner will be relatively rare.

Similar disintermediation will occur with lawyers, real estate agents, accountants, financial advisors—you get the picture. Virtually every sector of the global economy will experience some sort of "disintermediation" by technology, specifically artificial intelligence, neural networks, deep learning, big data . . . and whatever the newest lexicon calls it.

Now, it's not all bad!

We will have more time for leisure activities. A basic minimum income will probably be mandated by government, since work will largely be done by intelligent machines, on which there will be a tax.

The remaining jobs will also have to become more efficient, since many will be competing against "smart machines," artificial intelligence-based hardware and software systems that can literally think.

Efficiency will come from better collaborations, rich information sharing, real-time analytics, and other advances.

Gartner Group calls this evolutionary ecosystem, "Work-Stream Collaborations," and it's only just beginning. A select few startup companies here in Silicon Valley are attempting to figure out what this means. One such startup recently raised funding on a $5 billion valuation!

Gartner estimates that work-stream collaboration software-based networks will grow worldwide at a compounded annual rate of 96 percent for the foreseeable future, making this the fastest growing area of the internet.
One such network is called Milnaa.com. Milnaa attempts to bring social media collaboration tools to enterprises in order to increase the efficiency of "teams." Since most work is done by teams—small and large—organizations will now be better able to manage work. Milnaa.com estimates that its efficiency-enhancing service can improve productivity by as much as 30 percent or more.

Various other services such as Slack and Quip are also providing efficiency-enhancing tools, albeit in a variety of ways. Some are centered on instant messaging; others, like Milnaa, offer powerful new tools, such as three-dimensional voice and screen sharing around the "channel"—much like a wall where participants engage in conversations, share files, and get work done.

Collaboratively Yours,

Steve Sudhir Chainani
(Silicon Valley, Bombay, and Connecticut)

Share the AHA messages from this book socially by going to
http://aha.pub/ContextualCollaborations.

Section I

Contextual Collaboration

To get more things done effectively and in less time, collaboration is important. What is contextual collaboration, and what part does it play in today's workforce?

1

The Future of Work is Contextual
Collaboration!
http://aha.pub/ContextualCollaborations
http://aha.pub/SteveChainani

_____

_____

_____

2

The future of work is predicated on
the evolution of tools that facilitate
collaboration within teams.
http://aha.pub/SteveChainani

_____

_____

_____

3

Collaboration's a relationship where all parties strategically cooperate to achieve objectives. @Wikipedia http://aha.pub/SteveChainani

_____

_____

_____

4

Context refers to the constraints of a communicative situation that influence language use. @Wikipedia via http://aha.pub/SteveChainani

_____

_____

_____

5

#ContextualCollaboration is facilitated
by having the platform to co-mingle your
personal & business life.
http://aha.pub/SteveChainani

_____

_____

_____

6

Machines collaborate via Internet of Things (IOT) with increasing efficiency to scale. Humans do the same.
http://aha.pub/SteveChainani

_____

_____

_____

7

You can enhance any form of day-to-day activity, whether a sport or hobby, thru a collaborative process.
http://aha.pub/SteveChainani

_____

_____

_____

8

People always find ways to collaborate with someone, whether it's online or offline. http://aha.pub/SteveChainani

_____

_____

_____

9

Create and Innovate, it's much more
rewarding than following by rote!
http://aha.pub/SteveChainani

_____

_____

_____

10

How can we make people more productive,
efficient, and satisfied with work and play?
http://milnaa.com
http://aha.pub/SteveChainani

_____

_____

_____

11

We can be more efficient and productive by using tech to both push and pull info at the same time. http://aha.pub/SteveChainani

_____

_____

_____

12

Communicate, Share, and Ideate = Higher
Earning Power!
http://aha.pub/SteveChainani

_____

_____

_____

13

Learn at an accelerated pace rather than
a limited one. Teach, learn, and grow!
#ContextualCollaboration
http://aha.pub/SteveChainani

_____

_____

_____

14

Efficiency happens when purpose is maximally applied to a series of tasks with dedicated tools and processes.
http://aha.pub/SteveChainani

_____

_____

_____

15

Imagine using technology effectively
to react to and administer global relief.
#ContextualCollaboration
http://aha.pub/SteveChainani

_____

_____

_____

16

If you can improve the things you do on a daily basis by 30-40%, your life will certainly be improved. http://aha.pub/SteveChainani

_____

_____

_____

17

A higher level of engagement leads to more satisfying and effective collaborations. Engage well! http://aha.pub/SteveChainani

_____

_____

_____

18

Go online! It brings you collaborations on a global scale in real time. http://aha.pub/SteveChainani

_____

_____

_____

19

Earning power is magnified when our daily tasks are done with focus, persistence, and teamwork! http://aha.pub/SteveChainani

_____

_____

_____

20

With online access, you have an unlimited repertoire of productivity tools at your fingertips! #BeProductive http://aha.pub/SteveChainani

_____

_____

_____

21

Want a more granular form of collaboration that is relevant to your client? #ContextualCollaboration http://aha.pub/SteveChainani

_____

_____

_____

22

Effective #ContextualCollaboration is about where people have conversations and share their output. http://aha.pub/SteveChainani

_____

_____

_____

23

#ContextualCollaboration is creating the right platform where you can do personal and business in one place.
http://aha.pub/SteveChainani

_____

_____

_____

24

#ContextualCollaboration is the enabling
core for innovation.
http://aha.pub/SteveChainani

25

It's #ContextualCollaboration that makes
rapid innovation happen.
http://aha.pub/SteveChainani

Share the AHA messages from this book socially by going to
http://aha.pub/ContextualCollaborations.

Section II

On Learning and Growing

Growing is one of the most fundamental goals of a business. Having a contextual collaboration platform that aids in learning and maximizes opportunities of growth can help business executives reach their goals.

26

Life is better when we share with other people. @happyabout
http://aha.pub/SteveChainani

_____

_____

_____

27

In anything we do in life, we learn and grow.
#ContextualCollaboration
http://aha.pub/SteveChainani

_____

_____

_____

28

Basic daily activities can be enhanced if a
collaborative process is created to further
what you're doing.
http://aha.pub/SteveChainani

_____

_____

_____

29

Truly productive people embrace eternal learning! http://aha.pub/SteveChainani

_____

_____

_____

30

Sharing makes people more productive, efficient, and satisfied with personal and business life. http://aha.pub/SteveChainani

_____

_____

_____

31

Teaching is now moving to a higher plane of working together and being more efficient and productive.
http://aha.pub/SteveChainani

_____

_____

_____

32

Do not expect to work as productively as the robots that will take away our jobs. Keep re-inventing yourself. http://aha.pub/SteveChainani

_____

_____

_____

33

Your whole learning process can be greatly accelerated. It'll take you to the current thinking. http://aha.pub/SteveChainani

_____

_____

_____

34

The 4-day work week will be upon us soon,
yet the challenge will be to remain
relevant as employees.
http://aha.pub/SteveChainani

_____

_____

_____

35

Google is a good source for getting info, but it's not a place to collaborate. Use info to collaborate! http://aha.pub/SteveChainani

_____

_____

_____

36

When you pull info from Google, marry that to the experts, get their feedback, and learn from them. #ContextualCollaboration! http://aha.pub/SteveChainani

_____

_____

_____

37

Today, you can pull info from sources, share it with experts, and learn iteratively in almost real time.
http://aha.pub/SteveChainani

_____

_____

_____

38

You can learn from some of the best in the world online. Are you collaborating contextually? http://aha.pub/SteveChainani

_____

_____

_____

Share the AHA messages from this book socially by going to
http://aha.pub/ContextualCollaborations.

Section III

Engagement in Contextual Collaboration

In the past, engagement with other people was limited. Apart from meeting face-to-face, there was no other way to collaborate with people from across the globe. However, with the evolution of technology and the internet, we now have a way to communicate and engage anytime, anywhere.

39

Technology gives you the ability to do things and collaborate in real time on a global scale. http://aha.pub/SteveChainani

_____

_____

_____

40

Online, collaboration is not limited by any geographical or any physical means.
http://aha.pub/SteveChainani

_____

_____

_____

41

If you're having parallel conversations, that's parallel learning.
http://aha.pub/SteveChainani

_____

_____

_____

42

To drive a flying car, we'll need twice the
brain capacity we have today. You ready?
http://aha.pub/SteveChainani

_____

_____

_____

43

The amount of brain cells used today is astronomical. Our brains are going to have to grow. http://aha.pub/SteveChainani

_____

_____

_____

44

As we move to higher levels of engagement, we're just going to have to be smarter people. http://aha.pub/SteveChainani

_____

_____

_____

45

Collaboration is a composition of all known info to produce better outcomes.
http://aha.pub/SteveChainani

_____

_____

_____

46

Be flexible to career change...our world evolves at an ever more rapid rate!
http://aha.pub/SteveChainani

_____

_____

_____

47

The efficiency of mfg & services will be so high, we won't need to work > 4 days a wk, 4-6 hours a day.
http://aha.pub/SteveChainani

48

Machines and computers will soon augment your output, so you're not going to need to work that much.
http://aha.pub/SteveChainani

49

Having ADD is an extension component of being an innovator, leader, and inventor.
http://aha.pub/SteveChainani

_____

_____

_____

50

ADD means having multiple streams of thought held with intensity for a short time. http://aha.pub/SteveChainani

_____

_____

_____

51

ADD, if applied correctly, will lead to better innovation, creativity, output, and satisfaction. http://aha.pub/SteveChainani

_____

_____

_____

Share the AHA messages from this book socially by going to
http://aha.pub/ContextualCollaborations.

Section IV

Young vs. Old Generation

The young generation and the old generation have many differences, especially in the workplace. The latter was brought up in an authoritative model, while the former revolves around engagement and collaboration. It's inevitable that these two distinctive paths will collide at some point. How can the young generation and the old generation work together through contextual collaboration?

52

Instead of disparate systems, why not a unified system where all info can be filtered and made useful?
http://aha.pub/SteveChainani

_____

_____

_____

53

Imagine ALL forms of communicative
interactivity coming together in one place.
More efficient?
http://aha.pub/SteveChainani

_____

_____

_____

54

Increasing productivity and efficiency is crucial in the workplace. How? Aggregate multiple info sources.
http://aha.pub/SteveChainani

_____

_____

_____

55

A unified system enhances your efficiency by 30-40%, sometimes more!
http://aha.pub/SteveChainani

_____

_____

_____

56

There's room for a technology company to create a venue where multiple channels are located. http://aha.pub/SteveChainani

_____

_____

_____

57

The difference between the younger and the older generation is how they collaborate in the workplace. http://aha.pub/SteveChainani

_____

_____

_____

58

Today's generation wants instant gratification. They want info to be there in a fraction of a second.
http://aha.pub/SteveChainani

_____

_____

_____

59

Today, the complete cycle of getting info is massively compressed. What do you have access to? http://aha.pub/SteveChainani

_____

_____

_____

60

The availability of data today has risen exponentially. Are you taking advantage of this trend? http://aha.pub/SteveChainani

_____

_____

_____

61

Technology has been the driving force of the change in expectations between generations. http://aha.pub/SteveChainani

_____

_____

_____

62

Biggest difference between the old and new generation is the velocity of info flow and its application. http://aha.pub/SteveChainani

_____

_____

_____

63

Nowadays, we focus on products that get things done faster rather than on the brand itself. http://aha.pub/SteveChainani

---

64

The paradigm has shifted from being loyal to a brand to being loyal to a solution. http://aha.pub/SteveChainani #ContextualCollaboration

---

65

Innovation ecosystems evolve fast as the scope of disruption is high. Why? There's no loyalty to a brand!
http://aha.pub/SteveChainani

_____

_____

_____

66

All the problems we solve today, we solved yesterday; we just solved them in different industries & in different ways. @happyabout

_____

_____

_____

67

You need to understand both generations to take a model that worked in the past and make it work more effectively today.
@happyabout

_____

_____

_____

68

In the past decade, we've seen a normative shift in the fundamentals of thinking. What's about next decade?
http://aha.pub/SteveChainani

_____

_____

_____

69

The normative way of thinking has a half-life of 10 years and is getting shorter. Do you agree? http://aha.pub/SteveChainani

---

70

Every 10 years, 50% of what you consider normal is out the door. http://aha.pub/SteveChainani

---

71

Must we use different sets of tools for work & play? Or do they overlap because brands are irrelevant?
http://aha.pub/SteveChainani

_____

_____

_____

72

Toolsets have become sufficiently intelligent that they can straddle both the work and play domains.
http://aha.pub/SteveChainani

_____

_____

_____

73

Smart machines of the future can learn,
unlearn, relearn, and effectively broaden
their capabilities.
http://aha.pub/SteveChainani

_____

_____

_____

74

The massive impact machines create is
done with massive collaboration.
http://aha.pub/SteveChainani

_____

_____

_____

75

In the future, everything that's known in the world is actually collaborating with each other. http://aha.pub/SteveChainani

_____

_____

_____

76

IoT is just first generation. Imagine what the 10th generation will be like.
http://aha.pub/SteveChainani

_____

_____

_____

77

There will be machines that figure out how
to speedily process info and automatically
apply algorithms.
http://aha.pub/SteveChainani

_____

_____

_____

78

Define a problem, and the machine finds the info and the tools for you to solve it.
http://aha.pub/SteveChainani

_____

_____

_____

79

Future machines may even solve problems that you cannot define.
http://aha.pub/SteveChainani

_____

_____

_____

80

Future internet models can create venues for higher collaborations that lead to profitable outcomes.
http://aha.pub/SteveChainani

_____

_____

_____

81

We are at the rudimentary stages of creating the venues where higher-order thinking can be facilitated.
http://aha.pub/SteveChainani

_____

_____

_____

Share the AHA messages from this book socially by going to
http://aha.pub/ContextualCollaborations.

Section V

Channels for Contextual Collaboration

People need to have a way to collaborate contextually. With technology evolving by the minute, there are always new tools and platforms that connect people together and allow them to communicate, engage, and collaborate. What channels do businesses use for contextual collaboration?

82

How to have a dynamic play? Create channels for feedback and channels for delivering past content. @milnaa http://aha.pub/SteveChainani

_____

_____

_____

83

#ContextualCollaboration: Sports fans can learn from a two-way channel w/ the celebrity they're following. http://aha.pub/SteveChainani

_____

_____

_____

84

You can improve your game by watching past content. That's #ContextualCollaboration! http://aha.pub/SteveChainani

_____

_____

_____

85

#ContextualCollaboration allows both 1x1 private training and 2-way interactivity. http://aha.pub/SteveChainani

_____

_____

_____

86

Why not integrate cost control and convenience into the pervasive aspect of collaborating? @milnaa http://aha.pub/SteveChainani

_____

_____

_____

87

Technically, a collaboration platform may only be collaborative if money is made. @happyabout http://aha.pub/SteveChainani

_____

_____

_____

88

In #ContextualCollaboration, you can create a virtual league, say for baseball, and play a virtual game. http://aha.pub/SteveChainani

_____

_____

_____

89

An effective collaboration platform lets you do what you love while earning money. http://aha.pub/SteveChainani

_____

_____

_____

90

With #ContextualCollaboration, we have a way for retired sports figures to monetize the content they own.
http://aha.pub/SteveChainani

91

Satisfaction is now extremely important for businesses to scale and grow. What do you do to satisfy customers?
http://aha.pub/SteveChainani

92

We're launching a crusade to improve
humanity. An actual movement.
@milnaa http://aha.pub/SteveChainani

_____

_____

_____

93

We create channels for #ContextualCollaboration that makes us crusaders for change. @Milnaa http://aha.pub/SteveChainani

_____

_____

_____

94

Instead of calling it work, call it satisfaction.
#ContextualCollaboration
http://aha.pub/SteveChainani

_____

_____

_____

Share the AHA messages from this book socially by going to
http://aha.pub/ContextualCollaborations.

Section VI

Collaboration in Government

The government has been around for ages, even before technological innovations were operating. With times changing fast, government services need to improve their systems and processes to better serve the people. How can the government enhance itself to keep up?

95

We have a mechanism to improve local government through permit management process. @Milnaa
http://aha.pub/SteveChainani

_____

_____

_____

96

In India, Parliamentarians have a way to communicate achievements to voters.
@milnaa
http://aha.pub/SteveChainani

_____

_____

_____

97

Contractors & people in government used @Milnaa to collaborate & address pain points to implement projects.
http://aha.pub/SteveChainani

98

Screen sharing is now being used by engineers on the project site to collaborate more effectively.
http://aha.pub/SteveChainani

99

Govs will have an end-to-end solution that will help legislators facilitate governance for constituents. http://aha.pub/SteveChainani

_____

_____

_____

100

The same project can propagate thru diffrnt channels; teams work on differrent project aspects in isolation.
http://aha.pub/SteveChainani

_____

_____

_____

101

With multidimensional
#ContextualCollaboration, you can work on
a project better and faster.
http://aha.pub/SteveChainani

102

In #ContextualCollaboration, there's a
multi-dimensional facet to the whole aspect
of collaboration.
http://aha.pub/SteveChainani

103

There are methodologies of privacy & rules of engagement in sharing projects through different channels.
http://aha.pub/SteveChainani

_____

_____

_____

104

What will you be using collaboration for? What's the collaboration that's relevant for you? @happyabout http://aha.pub/SteveChainani

---

105

There are now dedicated apps in broad platform that include social media and enterprise collaboration. http://aha.pub/SteveChainani

---

Share the AHA messages from this book socially by going to
http://aha.pub/ContextualCollaborations.

Section VII

Platforms for Nonprofit Organizations

Like other types of organizations, nonprofits also contribute to society, which is why they have a need for contextual collaboration platforms. In truth, there are only a few out there that help these organizations to collaborate. Where can nonprofits find the right platform for them to work more effectively?

106

There aren't too many info platforms that help nonprofits publish their stuff. @Milnaa does. http://aha.pub/SteveChainani

_____

_____

_____

107

There is no real platform for a non-profit to collaborate with the entire world.
http://aha.pub/SteveChainani

_____

_____

_____

108

Milnaa provides non-profits a platform for patient-to-patient conversation.
#ContextualCollaboration
http://aha.pub/SteveChainani

_____

_____

_____

109

Wouldn't it be great if there were many holistic ways people dealt with cancer? #ContextualCollaboration http://aha.pub/SteveChainani

_____

_____

_____

110

Emergency and disaster management is another key issue for #ContextualCollaboration. http://aha.pub/SteveChainani

_____

_____

_____

111

With @Milnaa, people can upload real-time videos during disasters for sharing to first responders. http://aha.pub/SteveChainani

_____

_____

_____

112

In disasters, @Milnaa becomes a two-way communication and collaboration platform. http://aha.pub/SteveChainani

_____

_____

_____

113

For small and medium enterprises, communication and collaboration with customers is possible with @Milnaa. http://aha.pub/SteveChainani

_____

_____

_____

114

For small and medium enterprises, there can be separate channels in @Milnaa for each type of customer.
http://aha.pub/SteveChainani

_____

_____

_____

115

Small and medium enterprises can't afford expensive software to install and migrate data to. #Simplify
http://aha.pub/SteveChainani

116

As the #ContextualCollaboration model evolves, small businesses will move up the food chain to large ones.
http://aha.pub/SteveChainani

117

In the near future, small and large organizations will be more monetizable.
http://aha.pub/SteveChainani

_____

_____

_____

118

Large companies want advanced data analytics and reporting, for on-site training and product enhancement.
http://aha.pub/SteveChainani

_____

_____

_____

119

With #ContextualCollaboration, small and medium enterprises can enhance their processes for maximum results.
http://aha.pub/SteveChainani

_____

_____

_____

Share the AHA messages from this book socially by going to
http://aha.pub/ContextualCollaborations.

Section VIII

Making Leaders

For businesses and organizations to succeed in its endeavors, they need effective leaders. Their goal is to get people to engage and collaborate with each other to improve the organization. But what makes a good leader, and what characteristics do they have?

120

#ContextualCollaboration makes life more efficient, making us financially richer. http://aha.pub/SteveChainani

_____

_____

_____

121

Leaders exhibit sound judgment from making well-informed decisions, consistently! http://aha.pub/SteveChainani

_____

_____

_____

122

Effective leaders collaborate contextually to improve the business, all while having fun.
http://aha.pub/SteveChainani

_____

_____

_____

123

Today's world needs effective government services for its people. Effective leaders = effective government.
http://aha.pub/SteveChainani

_____

_____

_____

124

Leaders weigh in all known facts, then arrive at conclusions; #ContextualCollaboration reduces error. http://aha.pub/SteveChainani

_____

_____

_____

125

If you are a leader, find your tool of choice to make you more effective. #ContextualCollaboration http://aha.pub/SteveChainani

_____

_____

_____

126

Get more work done with
#ContextualCollaboration platforms. Have
you tried one yet?
http://aha.pub/SteveChainani

_____

_____

_____

127

Choose a #ContextualCollaboration
platform that lets you work safely and
securely. What platform do you use?
http://aha.pub/SteveChainani

_____

_____

_____

128

There are two key contemporary issues in today's era: privacy and security. #ContextualCollaboration http://aha.pub/SteveChainani

---

129

Network for work in the presence of factual data = great leadership = #ContextualCollaboration. http://aha.pub/SteveChainani

---

130

Payroll taxes on robots will fund Minimum Basic Income. Winners learn, unlearn, and re-learn, embracing change.
http://aha.pub/SteveChainani

_____

_____

_____

131

When you share, share to improve.
#ContextualCollaboration
http://aha.pub/SteveChainani

_____

_____

_____

132

You improve, and then you get to a higher level of whatever it is you're trying to achieve. http://aha.pub/SteveChainani

_____

_____

_____

133

Know how to ask questions, and after you ask the right ones, know how to interpret the results. http://aha.pub/SteveChainani

_____

_____

_____

134

Take a whole idea into a higher plane of
learning, a higher plane of interactivity.
http://aha.pub/SteveChainani

_____

_____

_____

135

Nobody wants to sit in a room with 50 people learning about topics that aren't interesting to them.
http://aha.pub/SteveChainani

136

On @Milnaa, you can learn from some of the best in the world.
http://aha.pub/SteveChainani

137

Start an innovative business and laugh your
way to the bank! Innovation = Profits
http://aha.pub/SteveChainani

_____

_____

_____

138

Learn more and do more with an infinite number of collaborators. #ContextualCollaboration http://aha.pub/SteveChainani

_____

_____

_____

139

If you're in entertainment, #ContextualCollaboration gives a more satisfying experience. http://aha.pub/SteveChainani

_____

_____

_____

140

The whole concept of engagement is in the context. #ContextualCollaboration http://aha.pub/SteveChainani

_____

_____

_____

About the Author

Steve Sudhir Chainani is the founder and CEO of Milnaa Media Pvt. Ltd. (https://www.milnaa.com/). He is the founder of award-winning international technology firms across North America and Asia, spanning semiconductors, software and systems, ecommerce, and social media.

Steve has twenty-five years of relevant experience in start-ups, technology, marketing, finance, strategy, and leadership. His passion is creating forward-looking business models and then implementing advanced web-based platforms to deliver innovative solutions.

AHАthat™

AHAthat makes it easy to share, author, and promote content. There are over 40,000 quotes (AHAmessages™) by thought leaders from around the world that you can share in seconds for free.

For those who want to author their own book, we have time-tested proven processes that allow you to write your AHAbook™ of 140 digestible, bite-sized morsels in eight hours or less. Once your content is on AHAthat, you have a customized link that you can use to have your fans/advocates share your content and help grow your network.

➲ Start sharing: http://AHAthat.com

➲ Start authoring: http://AHAthat.com/Author

Hey, Did You AHАthat™?

Steve Chainani
AHAthat Author

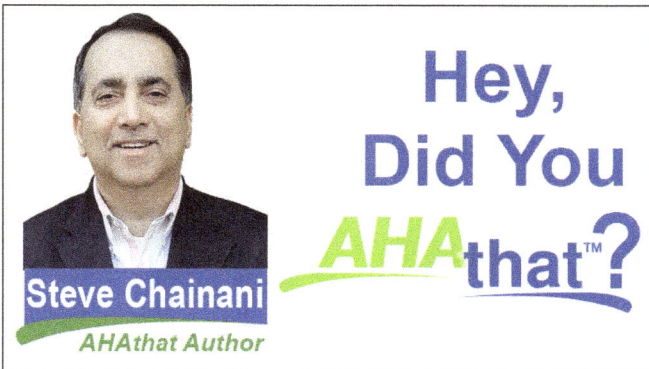

Please go directly to this book in AHAthat and share each AHAmessage socially at
http://aha.pub/ContextualCollaborations.